D0177809

Bristol Libraries
1806355875

ARMED SERVICES

Sarah Levete & Robert Snedden

W
FRANKLIN WATTS
LONDON•SYDNEY

Franklin Watts
First published in Great Britain in 2016 by The Watts Publishing Group

Credits
Series Editors: Sarah Eason and Jennifer Sanderson
Series Designers: Paul Myerscough and Simon Borrough

Picture credits: British Army: Crown Copyright 22, 26r; Department of Defense (DoD): 18, 23 right, 36, Airman 1st Class Corey Hook 13b, CPhoM. Robert F. Sargent, Coast Guard 27, Donna Miles 7r, Fred W. Baker III 24, Master Sgt. Scott Reed 3, Mike Kaplan U.S. Air Force 9, Petty Officer 2nd Class Christopher Vickers 38, Senior Airman Greg L. Davis 11, Sgt. Christopher S. Barnhart U.S. Army 5t, Staff Sgt. Aaron Allmon U.S. Air Force 1, Tech. Sgt. James L. Harper Jr. 14, Tech. Sgt. Jeremy T. Lock, U.S. Air Force 28, Tech. Sgt. Jeremy T. Lock U.S. Air Force 45; Dreamstime: Darrenw 5b, 21b, 23l, 25b, 26l, Edvard Molnar 33b, 35b, 37b, 39t, Yorrico 19, 29t, 31; MOD: Crown Copyright 4, 8; RAF: Crown Copyright 10, 15t, 20; Royal Navy: Crown Copyright 21, 25t, 32, 35t, 37; Shutterstock: aarrows 7l, 9b, 11b, 13t, 15b, Ksanawo 41b, 43, MarKord 29b; US Air Force: Staff Sgt. Marleah Robertson 17; US Army: Sgt. Timothy Kingston 30, Spc. Landon Stephenson 33t; US Marine Corps: MCIPAC Combat Camera Lance Cpl. Hernan Vidana 6; US Navy: Mass Communication Specialist 1st Class Eric L. Beauregard 40, Mass Communication Specialist 1st Class Talley Reeve 42; Wikimedia Commons LA(Phot) Keith Morgan 41t, Royal Navy/Crown Copyright 39b, Scott A. Thornbloom 34.

Dewey number: 355
ISBN: 978 1 4451 5041 3

Printed in China

Franklin Watts
An imprint of
Hachette Children's Group
Part of The Watts Publishing Group
Carmelite House
50 Victoria Embankment
London EC4Y 0DZ

An Hachette UK Company
www.hachette.co.uk

www.franklinwatts.co.uk

Contents

CHAPTER 1: The Armed Services

Who is trained to risk life and limb for their country? Who is prepared to use weapons to defend and protect others? Who will go on long tours of duty, far from home, living in rough-and-ready conditions? The answer to all these questions is the men and women in the army, navy and air force.

Together, a country's army, navy and air force make up its military or armed services. All areas of the armed services work together, but each one has a separate role, and their men and women have expertise in keeping their country and people safe.

Troops training

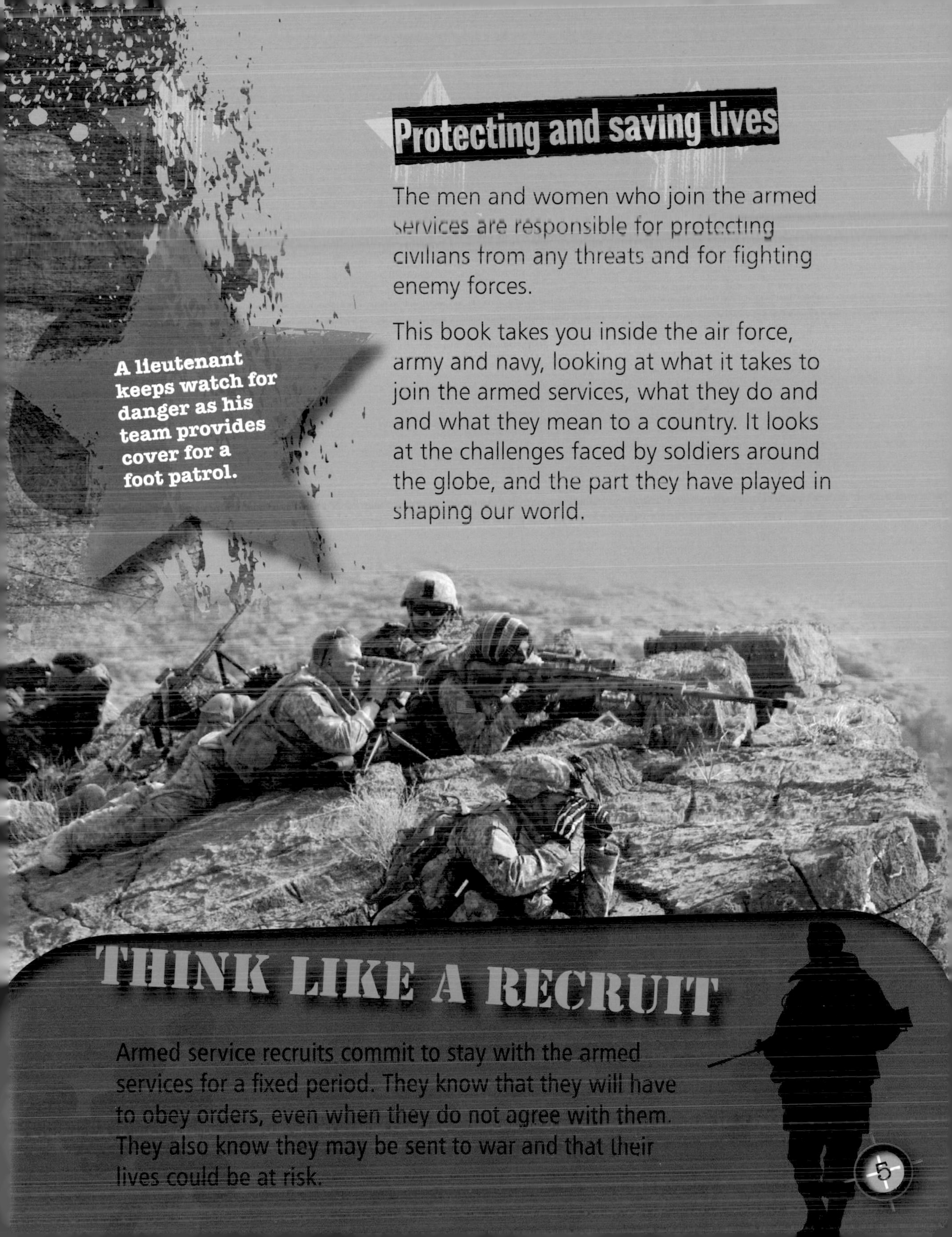

Protecting and saving lives

The men and women who join the armed services are responsible for protecting civilians from any threats and for fighting enemy forces.

This book takes you inside the air force, army and navy, looking at what it takes to join the armed services, what they do and and what they mean to a country. It looks at the challenges faced by soldiers around the globe, and the part they have played in shaping our world.

A lieutenant keeps watch for danger as his team provides cover for a foot patrol.

THINK LIKE A RECRUIT

Armed service recruits commit to stay with the armed services for a fixed period. They know that they will have to obey orders, even when they do not agree with them. They also know they may be sent to war and that their lives could be at risk.

CHAPTER 2: The Air Force

The air force's main mission is to conduct warfare from the air. The air force must protect its country from attack and it must be ready to attack the country's enemies.

The air force has many different responsibilities, including gaining control of the air (and so preventing attacks on its own country by enemy aircraft) and attacking enemy targets. It also supports ground troops by flying in supplies or providing covering fire. A country's air force may also be used to airlift supplies to disaster zones both at home and abroad.

Vital supplies are flown in to help the victims of the 2015 earthquake in Nepal.

Its role

In many countries, the air force is responsible for deploying and operating ground-based air defences, such as anti-aircraft guns and air-to-air missiles. The air force may also operate early warning networks and defensive systems, guarding against ballistic missile attacks. Some nations, such as Russia, have an Aerospace Defence Force, which is a military organisation separate from its air force.

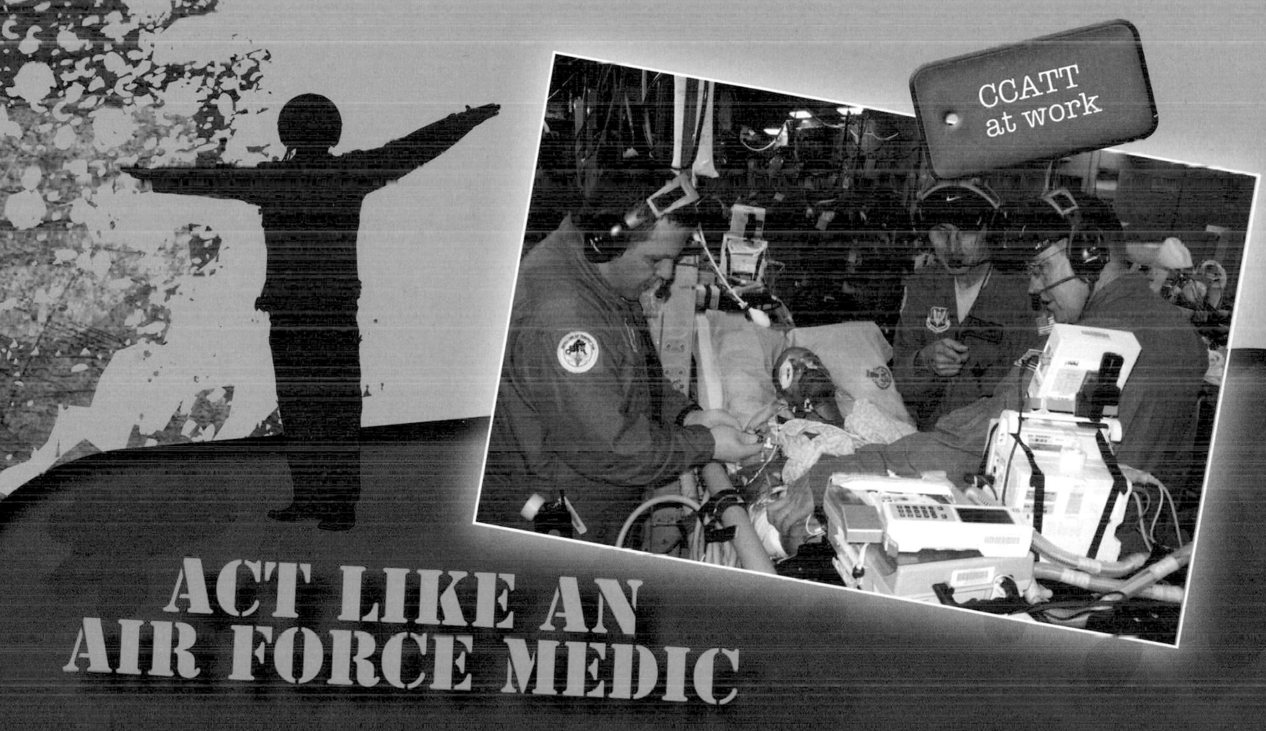

CCATT at work

ACT LIKE AN AIR FORCE MEDIC

A Critical Care Air Transport Team, or CCATT, is a specialised medical team. The team works with a transport aircraft and its crew to create an airborne intensive care unit, which flies critically ill patients or wounded soldiers to hospital. After an earthquake hit Haiti in 2010, CCATTs worked to transport victims to hospitals in Florida, United States, where they could get the help they needed.

Air Crew

Pilots fly combat jets, transport aircraft or helicopters. They perform many tasks. Some conduct air-to-air combat or ground attack missions, while others fly support aircraft to deliver supplies for ground troops or humanitarian aid. Helicopter pilots may take troops into combat or carry out search-and-rescue missions.

Recruitment for the air force varies from country to country. The air force looks for all-rounders – those who do well academically and in sporting activities. Air force officers need to be able to adapt to new situations quickly, they need to think logically and make decisions confidently. They also need a wide range of interests and abilities.

A Lynx helicopter delivers aid to North East Panay in the Philippines, following Typhoon Haiyan.

Being fit is an important part of being in the air force. Recruits must be fit enough to complete the initial and specialist training. To assess fitness, every candidate undergoes fitness tests: Selection Fitness Test, Pre-joining Fitness Test or Pre-recruit Training Course. The requirements for these tests depend on the role, age and gender of the recruit.

Officer training

Airmen and women make up the majority of the air force. Once they have gained experience and expertise, they can become officers. Officers are the equivalent to management. To become an officer, candidates must complete officer training.

Fit and ready

THINK LIKE AN OFFICER

Officer training puts the pressures of leadership and command on trainees by asking them to demonstrate what they have learnt with new recruits, and by leading their peers through various exercises. In order to advance, candidates will have to pass rigorous individual leadership evaluations.

Into Action

Fighter pilots are the elite of the air force. Becoming a fighter pilot requires dedication – the selection and training process can take years. Fighter pilots need to be able to think under enormous pressure. They also need to be physically very fit to deal with the stresses of high-speed air-to-air combat.

Those airmen and women who wish to train as fighter pilots fly fast jets or helicopters. Fast-jet pilots conduct air-to-air combat or ground attack missions. Helicopter pilots' duties range from ferrying troops into combat to search-and-rescue missions.

Air force pilots fly dangerous missions. This pilot is training for deployment to Afghanistan.

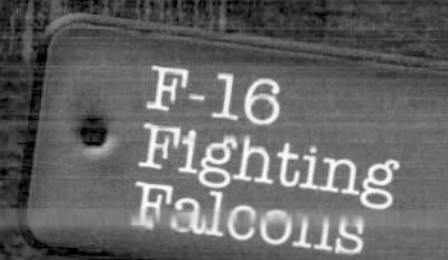

Dogfighting

One of the main skills a fighter pilot has to learn is dogfighting. A dogfight is an aerial combat between fighter aircraft. It is really important that the pilot does not lose sight of their enemy. Fighter pilots say, 'Lose sight, lose fight'. Air forces usually refer to a dogfight as air combat manoeuvring. Pilots are trained to make full use of the electronic warfare system when they are under attack.

ACT LIKE A FIGHTER PILOT

Pilots have to be fit to fight. Fighter pilots accelerating and making tight turns can experience massive G-forces. The force of 1 G is the equivalent to the gravity a person feels standing on the ground. A force of 2 G would make the person feel twice as heavy as they do normally. Fighter pilots can regularly experience forces of up to 9 G. They need to have strong muscles and healthy hearts to cope with this.

Ground Support

Aircraft technicians specialise in the maintenance of an air force's aircraft. They ensure the high performance of the aircraft's engines and flying controls. Their job is also to maintain all mechanical, structural and electrical parts of the aircraft.

An aircraft spends much more time on the ground than it does in the air. The ground equipment crew uses this time to service the aircraft's electrical and mechanical systems, repairing and replacing anything that looks like it might cause a problem when on a mission. They know it is far better to find a problem on the ground than in the air, so their work is done with great care and attention to detail.

Fixing aircraft

Aircraft technicians who repair the complicated avionics systems on board aeroplanes start as aircraft maintenance mechanics. After two years, they undergo avionics training to become aircraft technicians. As specialists in avionics, these technicians are responsible for the maintenance of radar, communications, reconnaissance and target-acquisition equipment. They also repair the onboard systems that control weapons.

THINK LIKE AN AIRCRAFT TECHNICIAN

An aircraft technician has to make sure that an aircraft is ready to fly at a moment's notice. The crew of the aircraft is completely dependent on the aircraft technician for making sure that every system is maintained to the highest standards. The integrity of the plane, and with it, the safety of the pilot and crew come down to the skills and attention to detail of the aircraft technician.

This technician is working to get a B1-B Lancer bomber ready for its mission.

Transport and Logistics

The job of the air force is not only to engage an enemy directly. Transport aircraft carry out the important task of supplying the equipment and personnel needed to maintain combat aircraft operating away from their home base. They also help to transport ground troops and the materials they need to fight effectively.

Air transport specialists make sure that food, water, medical supplies and combat equipment are transported safely and quickly to troops on the ground. Part of their training includes the safe handling of hazardous, or dangerous, materials. It is their job to ensure that the cargo is loaded and secured safely.

A Nepalese serviceman working for the United Nations ensures the safety of an airdrop. This airdrop of aid supplies took place after a hurricane hit Haiti in 2010.

Loading cargo

Logistics

Logistics officers are the airmen and women who manage the movement of the people, vehicles and equipment necessary to keep aircraft flying. They ensure that everyone is in the right place at the right time and that each person has the equipment that they need to do their job well, both at home and abroad. Their job includes buying and storing equipment and fuel, and organising the distribution of it.

THINK LIKE A LOGISTICS OFFICER

The air force has billions of pounds worth of equipment, from state-of-the-art fighters to spanners. However, none of it is of use if it is not where it should be. Keeping track of everything, and ensuring it all gets to the right place at the right time, is the job of the logistics officer. Logistic officers make sure that aircrews around the world get what they need to support their missions.

TAKE THE TEST!

Do you have what it takes to join the air force?

Trainees have to remember a lot of information to pass their tests. Check your knowledge with these questions:

Q1. What are the three branches of the armed services?

Q2. What is the main mission of the air force?

Q3. What does CCATT stand for?

Q4. Who are the 'managers' of the air force?

Q5. What are avionics technicians responsible for?

Q6. Who ensures that air force equipment is in the right place at the right time?

Q7. Who conducts air-to-air combat?

ANSWERS

Q1. The air force, army and navy

Q2. To conduct warfare in the air

Q3. Critical Care Air Transport Team

Q4. The officers

Q5. Maintenance of radar, communication, reconnaissance and target acquisition equipment

Q6. Logistics officers

Q7. Fast-jet pilots

CHAPTER 3: The Army

The men and women who join the army love the unexpected, working in different places and having a career in which no day is the same. The army, during peacetime or a conflict, is hard work but rewarding.

An army is a huge organisation. The British Army consists of the General Staff and the deployable Field Army and the Regional Forces that support them. There is also the Army Reserve that supports the regular army. The Army Reserve is made up of men and women who train for the army but keep their civilian jobs. They may be called into action if there is a war. Officers lead and give orders to enlisted soldiers. Enlisted soldiers carry out orders and perform specific duties.

Today, in many of the world's armies, women have opportunities in combat roles similar to those of male soldiers.

Rank and file

Each country's army is organised in a different way. A typical structure is:

★ **Officer Cadet:** rank held during initial officer training

★ **Second Lieutenant:** responsible for leading up to 30 soldiers in a platoon or troop, both in training and on operations

★ **Lieutenant:** normally commands a platoon or troop of around 30 soldiers

★ **Captain:** normally made second-in-command of a sub-unit of up to 120 soldiers

★ **Major:** can be given command of a sub-unit of up to 120 officers and soldiers

★ **Lieutenant Colonel:** commands units of up to 650 soldiers, containing four or five sub-units

★ **Colonel:** not usually a field commander. He or she serves as a staff officer between field commands at battalion/brigade level

★ **Brigadier:** commands a brigade or may be a director of operational capability groups, such as a director of staff

★ **Major General:** commands formations of division size

★ **Lieutenant General:** commands formations of corps size and other commands

★ **General:** the most senior appointment

ACT LIKE A CADET

Officer cadet is the lowest British Army officer rank. Cadets can work their way up through the army but it takes patience and discipline. Cadets have to learn the basics of the army during their training. During training they are tested to ensure that they have what it takes to move up the army ranks.

Army Life

Not everyone in the army wants to fight on the frontline. A huge range of roles is required to keep the army ready to defend and protect its country. Everyone who joins the army goes through basic training. Then, soldiers train in specialist areas, such as infantry or communications.

A team supports soldiers on the frontline, providing weapons and food as well as data and communications.

Camping out

An overseas army base or camp must be set up entirely from scratch. It takes many people to manage this job. The recent war in Afghanistan drew in troops from around the world to fight the Taliban. In the desert area of southern Afghanistan, British soldiers set up camp.

Camp Bastion

The camp began with a few tents, but within a couple of years, it had become a huge fortified base. At 41 square kilometres, it was the size of a small town. Camp Bastion was home to about 28,000 men and women. It had its own water bottling plant, airstrip, hospital and police force. Three huge dining halls were built, each able to feed about 7,000 people. If soldiers did not want the army food, they could get a takeaway from Bastion's KFC or Pizza Hut.

THINK LIKE AN ARMY CHEF

It is up to army chefs to make sure that the men and women in combat zones or in barracks are well fed. Sometimes, this means feeding hundreds of soldiers at a time. Chefs work in well-equipped kitchens with good supplies of food. In a war zone, however, chefs will work in a tented kitchen and must think creatively about how to use supplies to produce nourishing and energising food for exhausted soldiers.

Training

At any time, soldiers might find themselves trekking across rugged mountains through enemy territory, working in scorching temperatures to deliver aid packages or carrying a wounded comrade to safety. Excellent fitness is essential for these challenging situations. The tough army training begins when men and women apply to join. It continues throughout their career to ensure they are fit enough to carry out their tasks.

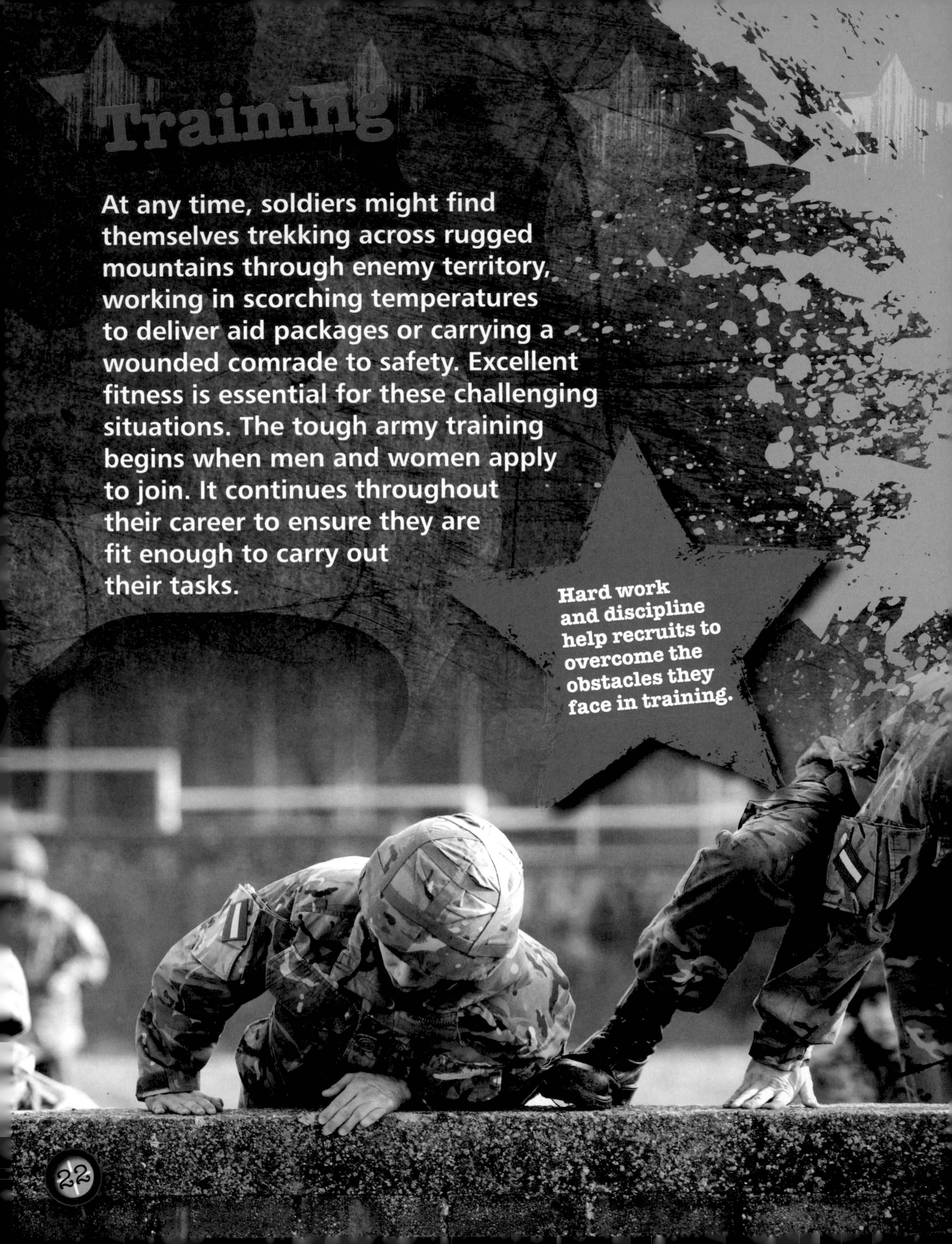

Hard work and discipline help recruits to overcome the obstacles they face in training.

Basic army training focuses on physical and practical skills, and making sure trainees have the right attitude to become a reliable member of the army. Training is often known as 'boot camp', during which recruits have to prove their physical fitness. They also have to show they can follow orders and work together as a team. Corporals constantly bark instructions and criticisms. The idea is to make sure that recruits can follow orders. This is crucial in highly stressful and chaotic situations during war.

A long, hard day

A typical day starts with an early wake up. Barracks must be tidied and cleaned. After a quick breakfast, soldiers do some form of physical exercise, which often involves running with heavy equipment. Further training may include learning to fire weapons, outdoor survival and map-reading skills. There is a short time after dinner to wind down before getting ready for more training the next day.

Morning workout

ACT LIKE A TRAINEE

At the start of training, new recruits hand over their personal belongings and are issued with army kit. Home for the next few weeks is the barracks, which recruits are expected to keep thoroughly clean. Recruits have to follow orders given to them by corporals. The non commissioned officers (NCOs) push recruits to the limit, physically and mentally.

Army Gear

During a conflict, soldiers might face sophisticated weapons or random homemade devices like improvised explosive devices (IEDs). The army has an armoury of powerful weapons, from grenades to heavy machine guns. Armoured fighting vehicles are equipped with protection against hostile attacks and often have weapons attached.

Land and air

Combat vehicles provide armoured protection against rocket-propelled grenades, and are fitted with a mobile gun system. Special army aircraft can transport combat vehicles to soldiers in the field. Modern armies also use unmanned aerial vehicles (UAVs). These drones are used for reconnaissance, surveillance, target acquisition and battle damage assessment. The RQ-7 Shadow is used by the Australian Army as well as the Swedish Army and the US Marine Corps.

Armoured vehicles can transport troops and provide covering fire.

Apache attack helicopters fly night and day, whatever the weather. An Apache can detect and identify up to 256 possible targets in seconds. Rockets, missiles and other weapons are carried on board.

Nuclear threat

In 1945, the United States dropped two nuclear weapons on the enemy Japanese cities of Hiroshima and Nagasaki. These bombs forced the Japanese to surrender, and brought World War II to a close. However, tens of thousands of people were killed and suffered horrific long-term effects as a result of the bombs. Since then, no other nation has used a nuclear bomb, although some countries, including the United States, the United Kingdom, Russia, India and Pakistan have nuclear weapons.

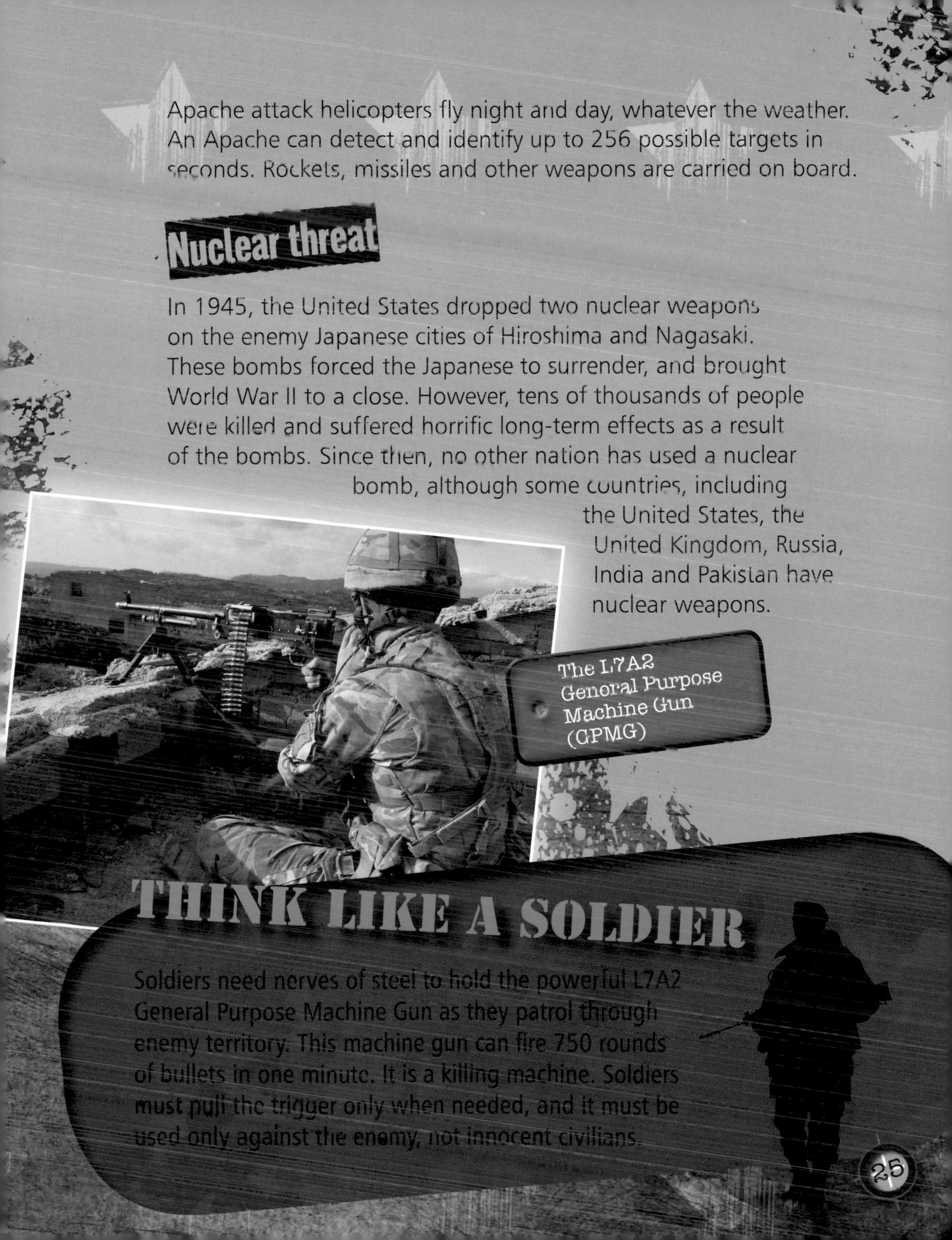

The L7A2 General Purpose Machine Gun (GPMG)

THINK LIKE A SOLDIER

Soldiers need nerves of steel to hold the powerful L7A2 General Purpose Machine Gun as they patrol through enemy territory. This machine gun can fire 750 rounds of bullets in one minute. It is a killing machine. Soldiers must pull the trigger only when needed, and it must be used only against the enemy, not innocent civilians.

War and Peace

The military's key mission is to defend its country and its country's interests, but armies work on crucial peacetime missions, too. These include rescue operations and support in humanitarian disaster crises. The Indian Army even built the world's highest bridge, a prefabricated Bailey bridge, in the Himalayan mountains, in 1982.

On patrol

THINK LIKE A SOLDIER

In most countries, soldiers sign up to the army for a set period. For example, in the British Army, soldiers can sign up for 12 years. Soldiers can leave if they are found unfit and cannot perform duties, or if they are unable to adapt to military life. Soldiers are expected to carry out orders during any conflict the army engages in, whether or not they agree with their country being at war.

The cost of war

Men and women in the army know that if their country is involved in a conflict or war they will be called upon to fight. Everyone who is sent on a mission risks injury and death. Added to military deaths are civilian deaths. For example, during World War II, about 40 million civilians died.

World War II led to the deaths of more than 20 million people serving in the military.

The Vietnam War

The Vietnam War took place from 1954 to 1975 between North Vietnam and the United States and South Vietnam. Several other counties, including Australia and New Zealand, sent in troops, too. The war was fought in unknown, hostile territory. However, the troops were unprepared for fighting in the dense North Vietnamese jungle. The death toll was high – in total, more than 58,000 men and women from the United States' armed forces, 521 Australians and 37 New Zealand soldiers died. Many soldiers became unhappy with the huge loss of life, and the length of the war against a seemingly unconquerable enemy. Around 5 per cent of US soldiers deserted the army during the war.

War on Terror

An army is a powerful organisation with well-trained soldiers and dangerous weaponry. It is essential that an army is organised and checked to make sure individuals work to defend and protect the interests of their country, not the interests of just a few. An armed group, however, has no such structure and does not have to justify its actions to a government. In some parts of the world, armed groups pressurise children to fight for them. These young children are then forced to carry out terrible deeds.

Armies are often active within their own countries, defending it from terrorist threats. The Kenyan Army is struggling to cope with the threat from the extremist group al-Shabaab. This group is responsible for many recent killings in Kenya, including an attack on a university campus in which 147 people were killed.

Different armies can share their expertise and skills. Here, US soldiers help train Kenyan soldiers.

THINK LIKE A COUNTER-INTELLIGENCE OFFICER

It is essential to stop an enemy from discovering the army's plans. A counter-intelligence officer makes sure that computer systems are secure. During a conflict, civilians who work on an army base must be checked to make sure they are not passing information to the enemy.

Terrorism

The world faces increasing threats from extremist groups. Armies work alongside other branches of the armed forces to counter the danger from these groups. Special Forces units are often important in this role. In Afghanistan, the US and British armies tackled the threat of terrorism with direct action, attacking the Taliban. The armies also tried to win over local people, persuading them not to support the terrorists. They did this by helping to build up the local area with essential services such as medical care and education. Could this be the way forward for armies to defeat the terrorist threat?

On alert in Paris

TAKE THE TEST!

Do you have what it takes?

Use the knowledge you have gained by reading this chapter to take this test:

Q1. What is the lowest British Army officer rank?

Q2. How many army personnel lived at Camp Bastion?

Q3. What does UAV stand for?

Q4. What drone is used by the Australian Army?

Q5. How many rounds can an L7A2 GPMG fire in one minute?

Q6. How many of the New Zealand Army's soldiers lost their lives in the Vietnam War?

Q7. What are barracks?

Q8. Boot camp is where the soldiers' boots are kept and cleaned. True or false?

Q1. Officer cadet

Q2. 28,000

Q3. Unmanned aerial vehicle

Q4. RQ-7 Shadow

Q5. 750

Q6. 37

Q7. Where recruits live and train to join the army

Q8. False. It is the informal name for the US Army-training period

CHAPTER 4: The Navy

Modern navies are huge organisations with thousands of men and women serving in their ranks. As well as staff, navies have combat ships and a number of other support vessels such as minesweepers, patrol craft and hospital ships.

In addition to its ships, a navy also includes a fleet of aircraft that may be stationed on board aircraft carriers or on land. Modern naval combat ships can be divided into seven types: aircraft carriers, cruisers, destroyers, frigates, corvettes, submarines and amphibious assault ships. Support and auxiliary ships include minesweepers, patrol boats, survey ships, tenders and oilers.

Aircraft carrier

The hospital ship *USNS Comfort* sails on an humanitarian mission to Haiti in 2009.

Units

A navy's forces can be deployed in a variety of units, based on the number of ships involved. For example, the smallest operational unit is just a single ship. Ships may be combined to form squadrons of between three and ten vessels. A squadron can be made up of just one type of ship or several. For example, in the US Navy, a squadron is usually a formation of destroyers and submarines. A fleet is the largest-sized unit – the equivalent of an army on the land. For a smaller country, a fleet may be its whole navy. A task force is a fleet of ships that has been specially put together to carry out a mission.

THINK LIKE A TASK FORCE COMMANDER

When Argentina invaded the Falkland Islands in 1982, the British government put together a task force to retake them. The nuclear submarine HMS *Conqueror* was first to set out on 4 April, and the aircraft carriers HMS *Invincible* and HMS *Hermes* soon followed. The whole task force eventually totalled 127 ships, including 43 Royal Navy vessels, 22 Royal Fleet auxiliary ships and 62 merchant ships (including the ocean liners SS *Canberra* and *Queen Elizabeth II*, which were used as troop carriers).

Joining the Navy

Enlisted sailors are the workforce of the navy. They hold many different positions and responsibilities across the service.

To join the navy, recruits must meet certain criteria. Most navies have a minimum age limit. For example, Royal Navy applicants must be between 16 and 36 years old. Some navies also expect applicants to complete a pre-joining fitness test, which may include running a set distance within a specific time.

Before getting on board, new recruits complete basic training. This can take 10 weeks, depending on the country. Once the basic skills have been learnt, the recruits begin specialist training for their chosen job aboard a ship. There are hundreds of different roles that the new recruits can train for in the navy, from submarine electronics to cyberwarfare engineers, explosive ordinance technicians and gunners' mates.

Female US Navy recruits are issued their new uniform.

Physical tests

All members of a navy have to be physically fit. To graduate from basic training, most navies require trainees to complete a physical fitness test. For example, these are just some of the exercises that the Royal Australian Navy requires sailors to complete before they can graduate: 25 push-ups, 25 sit-ups, 2.4 kilometre run in fewer than 13 minutes, 500 metre swim in fewer than 12.5 minutes.

Diving exercise

THINK LIKE A SAILOR

From the very first day of training, the navy teaches new recruits the value of teamwork. There is no job in the navy that does not depend on other sailors doing their job, too. Sailors learn to rely on the people they work alongside, and they make sure that others can count on them, too.

Patrolling in secret beneath the waves, the submarine fleet keeps watch on the ships and submarines of other nations. Some submarines carry nuclear missiles. These are the ultimate weapons of last resort. Submarines were first widely used during World War I, and today, they form an important part of many navies around the world.

Operating hundreds of metres below the sea, it is absolutely vital that members of a submarine crew know they can rely on each other. This means it is important to select the right people to serve in the submarine service. Candidates are thoroughly screened for suitability before going through training that may take up to one year, depending on the navy. At the end of training, most navies award their submariners with a special insignia (badge) to show that they have completed their submariner training.

The nuclear-powered attack submarine USS *Jimmy Carter* begins its sea trials off the coast of Connecticut, United States.

All navies are different but for many, a submariner's day is broken up into shifts. In the Royal Australian Navy, for example, each day is broken up into four six-hour shifts. During a submariner's six hours on-watch, he or she operates equipment and performs assigned tasks. For the six hours off duty, submariners can eat, sleep, read, exercise, watch television, study or play video games. To keep fit at sea, there are exercise bikes, rowing machines and free weights.

HMS Astute returns home

ACT LIKE A GUIDED MISSILE SUBMARINE COMMANDER

The commander of a guided missile submarine has a formidable weapon at his disposal. Armed with tactical missiles and superior communications, they are equally ready to spy or strike decisively. They are designed to serve and support the needs of special operations forces around the world. Each submarine has a lock-out chamber that allows special operations forces to enter and leave the submarine while it is submerged.

Shore Duties

A naval base is where ships are stationed when they have no active mission. At the ship's home port, the vessel can be resupplied and maintenance can be carried out.

A naval base is a tight-knit community. The base is like a town with everything, from shops and hospitals to police and fire stations. Often, there is a cinema and library, too.

The aircraft carrier *USS George Washington* leaves Naval Station Norfolk as it sets out on a new deployment.

HM Naval Base Devonport in England is the largest naval base in Western Europe. The site covers more than 2.6 square kilometres and has 15 dry docks, 6.4 kilometres of waterfront, 25 tidal berths and five basins. The base employs 2,500 Royal Navy personnel. Devonport is the home port of the Devonport Flotilla, which includes the largest ship in the Royal Navy – HMS *Ocean* – and the *Trafalgar*-class submarines.

ACT LIKE A MARINE ENGINEER OFFICER

The Royal Navy's marine engineer officers are responsible for maintaining the Navy's fleet both in port and on the water. They ensure that the fleet operates as it should, ensuring that each component is in perfect working order. If an emergency occurs, these officers are responsible for overseeing damage control and they report directly to the captain of the ship.

HMNB Devonport

Working Together

Ships from the navies of different countries sometimes join forces to accomplish a mission. Combined Maritime Forces (CMFs) is a naval partnership between several countries that aims to combat terrorism, prevent piracy and keep the oceans safe for shipping. The CMF also offers aid to the victims of natural disasters.

The CMF is commanded by a US Navy vice admiral and is based at US Naval Support Activity Bahrain. It is made up of three main combined task forces (CTFs):

- CTF-150: responsible for security and counter-terrorism
- CTF-151: responsible for counter-piracy
- CTF-152: ensures Arabian Gulf security

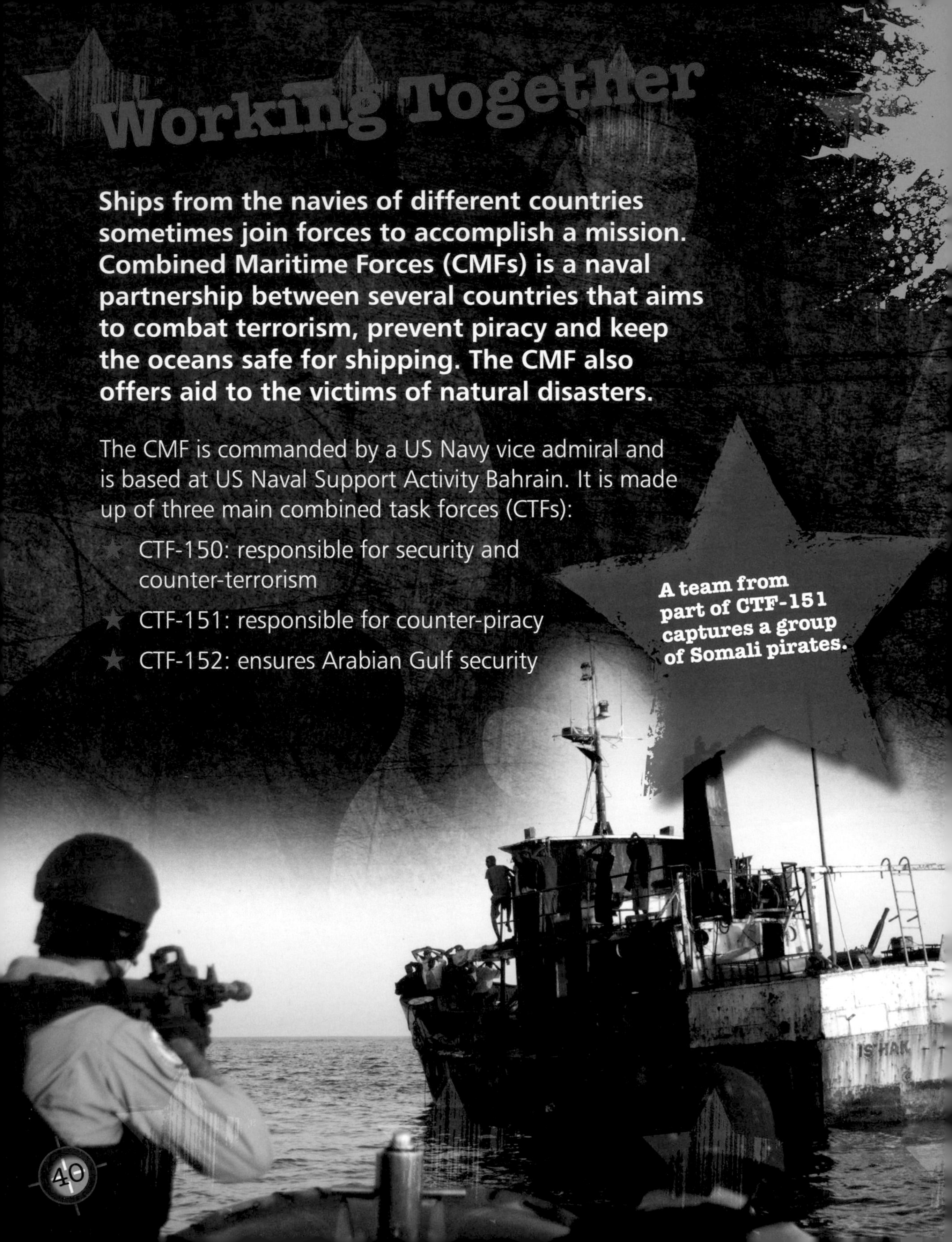

A team from part of CTF-151 captures a group of Somali pirates.

CTF-150

CTF-150's area of operation (AOR) spans the Red Sea, Gulf of Aden, Indian Ocean and Gulf of Oman. The safety of this area is vital for world trade because it includes the main shipping routes from the Far East to Europe and the United States.

Royal Navy destroyer from CT-150

ACT LIKE A CTF MEMBER

On 8 April, 2009, four Somali pirates took control of the US-flagged container ship *Maersk Alabama*. The crew members put up a fight and the pirates fled in one of the ship's lifeboats, taking Captain Richard Phillips captive. Fortunately for Phillips, ships of CTF-151 were nearby. The destroyer USS *Bainbridge* was the first to respond and reached the lifeboat on the night of 9 April. The destroyer used spotlights, loudspeakers and sirens to keep the pirates on edge while they awaited the arrival of SEAL Team 6, flying in from Virginia to make the rescue. Under cover of darkness, the SEALs parachuted into the ocean and climbed aboard the *Bainbridge*. From the deck of the ship, the SEALs used sniper fire to kill the pirates and set Phillips free, unharmed.

TAKE THE TEST!

Could you be a part of the navy?

Before you join the navy, you need to know a little more about it. How much do you remember from what you have just read?

Q1. Name three support vessels found in a navy.

Q2. How many ships make up a United States Navy squadron?

Q3. How old must Royal Navy applicants be?

Q4. In the Royal Australian Navy fitness test, how many push-ups must a recruit complete in order to pass the test?

Q5. When were submarines first used widely?

Q6. What is Western Europe's largest naval base?

Q7. What does CMFs stand for?

Q8. Where is the CMF based?

ANSWERS

Q1. Minesweepers, patrol craft and hospital ships

Q2. Between three and 10 vessels

Q3. Between 16 and 36 years old

Q4. 25

Q5. World War I

Q6. Devonport

Q7. Combined Maritime Forces

Q8. US Naval Support Activity Bahrain

Have You Got What it Takes?

Are you considering a career in the armed services? There are plenty of things you can start to do that will help prepare you for a military career.

Education

Study hard to get your qualifications. You need to have certain qualifications to join the armed services. Most officer jobs require a college or university qualification.

Volunteer

Join clubs and groups that offer you the chance to improve your fitness and develop your team skills. How about mentoring or supporting a group of younger children in a particular sport? Take the opportunity to lead and support schoolfriends. It will show your leadership qualities. Armed services roles often involve working with the community. Think about how you can help your local community, perhaps by offering to help raise funds for a local charity.

Consider Your Skills

Think about which specialism you would like to work in, such as combat, medicine or communications. Consider what area would best suit your personality and skills.

Fitness

It is essential you keep yourself in good physical shape. Take plenty of exercise and eat a healthy, balanced diet. Try out a range of exercises and make sure to include some team sports. Remember that teamwork is very important.

At Home

Talk to your parents or carers about your plans. It helps to have their support.

Self Discipline

Keep your room and school books organised. This will help to prepare you for the discipline and order needed for the armed services.

Personality

Make sure your behaviour and actions are always responsible and thought through. Armed services recruiters look for young men and women who can live by these values.

Glossary

ammunition the projectiles used in guns

aircraft carriers large warships from which aircraft can take off and land

amphibious able to operate on land or sea

ballistic missile short for intercontinental ballistic missile (ICBM), a missile with a range of more than 5,500 kilometres

barracks where recruits live and train to join the army

boot camp a training camp for new recruits

civilians people not in the military

commissioned officer an officer who trains for a leadership role immediately

deployment moving forces into a position of readiness

enlisted to have joined one of the armed services

fortified protected frontline close to the enemy

home port the port where a ship has its base

hostile enemy

humanitarian looking after the needs of people

infantry soldiers who fight mainly on foot

merchant ships civilian ships carrying passengers or cargo

minesweeper a ship equipped to detect and remove explosive mines

nuclear weapons bombs or missiles that use nuclear energy to cause incredibly destructive explosions

oiler a ship carrying fuel oil for other ships

reconnaissance observing an area to determine enemy activity

recruits people who have recently joined the military

squadron a group of warships

surveillance observation

tactical actions planned to gain a military advantage

Taliban an extremist Islamic group

target-acquisition the detection, identification, and location of a target, allowing it to be fired on if necessary

task force an armed force organised to carry out a particular objective

For More Information

Books

Armed Services (Edge – Action Force), Jim Bush, Franklin Watts

Soldier (DK Eyewitness), Simon Adams, Dorling Kindersley

World War II: Navy (Edge – Action Force), John Townsend, Franklin Watts

Websites

Have fun playing army-related games at this site:
www.militarykidsconnect.dcoe.mil/tweens/games

See video footage of the Royal Australian Navy in action by visiting:
http://video.navy.gov.au

Learn more about the equipment used by the Royal Air Force:
www.raf.mod.uk/equipment

Note to parents and teachers
Every effort has been made by the Publisher to ensure that these websites contain no inappropriate or offensive material. However, because of the nature of the Internet, it is impossible to guarantee that the contents of these sites will not be altered. We strongly advise that Internet access is supervised by a responsible adult.

Index